OCEAN
IT'S MY HOME!

Angela Royston

Crabtree Publishing Company

www.crabtreebooks.com

Author: Angela Royston
Editors: Kathy Middleton
Crystal Sikkens
Project coordinator: Kathy Middleton
Production coordinator: Ken Wright
Prepress technicians: Ken Wright
Margaret Amy Salter

Picture Credits:
Dreamstime: Tom Dowd: page 8; Halbrindley: page 19;
J. Henning Buchholz: page 15; Vladimir Seliverstov:
page 18; Tyneimage: page 20; Vladvitek: pages 1, 13;
Willtu: page 12
National Geographic: Norbert Wu/Minden
Pictures/N G Stock: page 11
Photolibrary: Franco Banfi: page 16; Corbis: page 21;
Doug Perrine: page 9; Wolfgang Poelzer: pages 3, 14;
Tom Soucek: page 17
Rex: Nature Picture Library: page 10
Shutterstock: cover; Rich Carey: page 6; Khoroshunova
Olga: page 5; Specta: pages 4, 7

Library and Archives Canada Cataloguing in Publication

Royston, Angela
Ocean it's my home! / Angela Royston.

(Crabtree connections)
Includes index.
ISBN 978-0-7787-7851-6 (bound).--ISBN 978-0-7787-7873-8 (pbk.)

1. Marine animals--Juvenile literature. 2. Marine ecology--
Juvenile literature. I. Title. II. Series: Crabtree connections

QL122.2.R675 2011   j591.77   C2011-900597-2

Library of Congress Cataloging-in-Publication Data

Royston, Angela, 1945-
Ocean it's my home! / Angela Royston.
p. cm. -- (Crabtree connections)
Includes index.
ISBN 978-0-7787-7873-8 (pbk. : alk. paper) --
ISBN 978-0-7787-7851-6 (reinforced library binding : alk. paper)
1. Ocean--Juvenile literature. 2. Marine ecology--Juvenile
literature. I. Title.
GC21.5.R687 2011
591.77--dc22
                                                    2011001330

Crabtree Publishing Company
www.crabtreebooks.com   1-800-387-7650

Printed in the U.S.A./042015/CG20150312

Published in Canada
Crabtree Publishing
616 Welland Ave.
St. Catharines, Ontario
L2M 5V6

Published in the United States
Crabtree Publishing
PMB 59051
350 Fifth Avenue, 59th Floor
New York, New York 10118

Contents

Water World

A lot of animals live in the **oceans**. Some are beautiful, others look very strange!

Swimming together

Lots of fish swim in the oceans. Some swim in huge groups, called **schools**.

Keep together!

It is safer to swim as a group.

Crab home

Some sea creatures, such as crabs, hide under the sand.

Reef Home

Lots of animals live around **coral reefs.** Coral looks like a plant, but it is made up of a lot of tiny animals.

coral

Scary stinger

Sea anemones live on coral reefs. They have **tentacles** that sting.

This coral looks like a cauliflower!

Clownfish

An anemone's tentacles sting fish – all except the clownfish.

Clownfish

Can't sting me!

Fantastic Fins

Fish use their **fins** to swim in their ocean home. Some fish have special fins.

Fish that fly

Flying fish use their fins to leap out of the sea and **glide** like a bird.

big fin ———————○

Flying fish can fly for 30 seconds.

We can fly!

big fin

Fastest fish

A sailfish swims really fast. It has a huge fin that looks like a sail.

In the Dark

Strange fish live at the bottom of the sea. It is always dark down here.

Look at my light!

An anglerfish uses its light to make curious fish swim closer. Then it gobbles them up.

An anglerfish makes its own light.

Big mouth

A **gulper eel** can swallow a fish that is bigger than itself!

light

Open wide!

11

Shark!

Sharks are speedy swimmers.
They hunt and eat fish and
other sea animals.

Killer shark

The great white shark is one
of the biggest and fastest sharks.
It is also one of the scariest!

fin

Great whites
have a
white belly.

white belly

Shiny new teeth

Every time a shark loses a tooth, a new one takes its place.

Scary shark

Water Wings

Rays are wide, flat fish.
They swim through water
by flapping their wings.

Giant ray

A ray has a long, thin tail. A giant
manta ray is the biggest ray of all.

We don't bite.

wing

tail

No teeth

Manta rays have no teeth. They swallow tiny sea animals.

A manta ray is big but harmless.

Ocean Giants

Whales are huge. Blue whales are the largest animals on Earth.

Coming up for air

Whales swim underwater, but they come up to the surface to breathe in air.

Sing along!

Big breath

Whales blow out air and water, then breathe in air.

Humpback whales sing as they swim.

Cold Home

Walruses live in cold and icy seas. They have lots of fat to keep them warm.

Long teeth

A walrus has two long teeth called **tusks.** It uses them to fight and to find food.

Walruses like to lie on ice.

Ice pick

A walrus uses its tusks to help it climb onto the ice.

Chill out!

Above the Sea

Some birds fly over huge oceans. If they get tired, they sleep as they fly!

Making a nest

Seabirds make nests on rocks and cliffs. They lay their eggs in them.

Puffins make nests on rocks.

Huge wings

Albatrosses glide for hours without moving their wings.

Rocky home

Glossary

albatrosses Very large seabirds

coral reefs Structures that feel like rock but are made of millions of tiny sea animals

fins Parts of a sea animal that stick out from the animal's body. A sea animal moves its fins to help it to swim.

glide Fly without moving the wings

gulper eel Deep-sea fish with a very big mouth and a stretchy stomach

oceans Huge areas of water

shoals Large groups of fish

tentacles Long feelers that a sea animal uses to move and to feel. Some tentacles contain stings.

tusks Two long teeth, one on each side of the mouth

Further Reading

Web Sites

This Web site gives lots of facts about sharks. Find it at:
www.enchantedlearning.com/subjects/sharks

You can listen to the song of a humpback whale at:
www.youtube.com/watch?v=xo2bVbDtiX8

Books

Earth's Oceans (Looking at Earth) by Bobbie Kalman, Crabtree Publishing (2008).

All About Sharks by Jim Arnosky, Scholastic (2008).

Wonderful Whales (The Living Ocean) by Bobbie Kalman, Crabtree Publishing (2006).

Skates and Rays (The Living Ocean) by Rebecca Sjonger and Bobbie Kalman, Crabtree Publishing (2006).

Index